CAMBRIDGE

CW01652460

GCSE ENGLISH LANGUAGE

Writing Workshops

Mike Ferguson and Martin Phillips

CAMBRIDGE
UNIVERSITY PRESS

University Printing House, Cambridge CB2 8BS, United Kingdom

Cambridge University Press is part of the University of Cambridge.

It furthers the University's mission by disseminating knowledge in the pursuit of education, learning and research at the highest international levels of excellence.

www.cambridge.org
Information on this title: www.cambridge.org/9781107526877 (Paperback)
www.cambridge.org/9781107526907 (Cambridge Elevate-enhanced Edition)
www.cambridge.org/9781107526860 (Paperback + Cambridge Elevate-enhanced Edition)

© Cambridge University Press 2015

This publication is in copyright. Subject to statutory exception and to the provisions of relevant collective licensing agreements, no reproduction of any part may take place without the written permission of Cambridge University Press.

First published 2015

Printed in the United Kingdom by Latimer Trend

A catalogue record for this publication is available from the British Library

ISBN 978-1-107-52687-7 Paperback
ISBN 978-1-107-52690-7 Cambridge Elevate-enhanced Edition
ISBN 978-1-107-52686-0 Paperback + Cambridge Elevate-enhanced Edition

Additional resources for this publication at www.cambridge.org/ukschools

Cambridge University Press has no responsibility for the persistence or accuracy of URLs for external or third-party internet websites referred to in this publication, and does not guarantee that any content on such websites is, or will remain, accurate or appropriate.

NOTICE TO TEACHERS IN THE UK

It is illegal to reproduce any part of this work in material form (including photocopying and electronic storage) except under the following circumstances:

(i) where you are abiding by a licence granted to your school or institution by the Copyright Licensing Agency;
(ii) where no such licence exists, or where you wish to exceed the terms of a licence, and you have gained the written permission of Cambridge University Press;
(iii) where you are allowed to reproduce without permission under the provisions of Chapter 3 of the Copyright, Designs and Patents Act 1988, which covers, for example, the reproduction of short passages within certain types of educational anthology and reproduction for the purposes of setting examination questions.

Contents

Introduction

Every day you write. In fact, you probably write quite a considerable amount because, in school, teachers in all subjects need you to write down details about what they are getting you to learn.

However, writing in the subject English is a bit different. English gives you the chance to write for the sake of it. Your English teacher will certainly try to help you write clearly and accurately, because that is a very important life skill – given high value by employers. However, English lessons will also encourage you to write creatively: to amuse yourself and others; to write passionately about things you think are important; to reflect on experiences that have happened to you and your family which have made you the person you are.

Watch Martin Phillips introduce the Writing Workshops on Cambridge Elevate.

THE CHOICE IS YOURS

This collection of Writing Workshops will help you improve your writing by honing your skills in a series of activities. The word 'workshop' has been carefully chosen. The *Cambridge Dictionary* gives two definitions for the word 'workshop':

1. a room or building where things are made or repaired using machines and/or tools
2. a meeting of people to discuss and/or perform practical work in a subject or activity.

Both the dictionary definitions apply to the writing workshops you will complete as part of your GCSE course. With a partner, write a sentence or two about how each definition can apply to writing in a classroom.

The workshops will help you to craft a whole series of different types of writing. You will write reviews, advertising material, imaginative descriptions, creative narratives, dialogues, screenplays, letters of complaint and more. These are called different writing 'forms' or 'genres' (a French word meaning 'category'). However, the differences between these forms will not be your main focus. Whatever you are writing, you will face the same set of choices:

Choice 1: Vocabulary. What words am I going to use to help my reader see things clearly?

Choice 2: Sentence structure. How can I craft my sentences so that they keep my reader interested?

Choice 3: Text structure. How can I build my whole piece of writing so that it takes my reader on a logical or exciting journey through what I want to say?

Some people make a living just by writing. They have to be good to do that, so you will look at many examples of the work of good writers – past and present. However, the main focus of the writing workshops is **you**. At the beginning of each workshop is a note explaining the specific skills you are covering.

Hopefully this will be just the beginning of the process, and you will continue writing for pleasure long after you have completed your GCSEs. Remember – the thing about becoming a writer is that you are never finished; there is always more to learn. As the American writer Ernest Hemingway said: 'We are all apprentices in a craft where no one ever becomes a master.'

Good luck!

Mike Ferguson and *Martin Phillips*

Writing workshop 1

Word power

Your writing improvement focus for this workshop will be:

- **communication:** improving your vocabulary
- **communication:** choosing words that have maximum impact on the reader.

One of the most important choices any writer makes is which words to use in their writing – especially their choice of **nouns**, **adjectives**, **verbs** and **adverbs**. These words are the key to successfully communicating to the reader the picture that the writer has in their own mind.

DISCUSSING

1. Work with another student. Describe to each other the picture that comes to mind when you read this sentence:

   The dog barked outside.

2. Write out the sentence, adding the extra words you used in your own description to give a more detailed picture of your barking dog. You may have described the type of dog, its colour and where it is, among other things. You will almost certainly have used more words than the original sentence.

3. How many different words to describe emotions or moods can you think of?

4. In one of his songs, Bob Dylan described a dog barking:

   Way out in the wilderness, a cold coyote calls.

   a What sort of mood or emotion do you think he wanted people to feel when hearing that line?
   b What are the most important words used to conjure up that feeling?
   c What might a song that included those lyrics be about?

DRAFTING

When words conjure up a particular image in a reader's mind, it is called **connotation**. This is an important idea to understand, because connotation is crucial to the impact your writing has on your reader.

5 Write three more sentences about dogs barking. In each one, try to make your reader feel a different emotion. For example you could try to convey loneliness, love for the animal, terror, annoyance.

DISCUSSING

Look at the names on the paint chart in Source A. The colours are not just called 'dark green' or 'creamy yellow' – the names have been chosen for their connotations.

6 Choose three or four of the names and discuss what connotations these words have for you. For example 'Whisper' might make you think of something secret and mysterious.

7 Look for ways to group some of the names and their connotations. Then discuss what type of person you think the designers of the paint chart had in mind when coming up with these names.

DRAFTING

8 Imagine you work in the marketing department of a paint manufacturer. Look at the paint colours on the chart in Source B. Choose three of them, then come up with a name for each one. You should try to target three different **audiences**:

- **a** Young men (aged 17–24) interested in sport.
- **b** Women aged 45–60 in professional jobs (doctors, solicitors, and so on).
- **c** Men or women aged 30–45 working in advertising or media.

Watch Lemn Sissay talk about the power of words on Cambridge Elevate.

Source A

Source B

WRITING

It is not only words that have connotations. Visual images may mean different things to different people, because pictures can trigger personal memories.

Look at the photograph in Source C. For someone who has just had a wonderful holiday, the connotations will be good ones – recalling sunny beaches and delicious food, for example. For someone returning from a bad holiday, with dirty, noisy accommodation and whose money had been stolen, the image will have very different connotations.

Source C

9 Work with another student. Choose one of the images in Source D. Write two sentences that capture the mood or **tone** of the picture. One should be a short sentence. The other should be a sentence that is rich in detail.

Think very carefully about the individual words you have chosen. Do not be content to go with the first ideas you have: look in a thesaurus for other words that might be more powerful.

10 When you have finished your writing, swap with another pair of students who have written about the same image. Discuss the word choices you have made.

- **a** Are there differences in the way you responded to the images?
- **b** What words make this most obvious?

Source D

Writing workshop 2

Setting the scene

Your writing improvement focus for this this workshop will be:

- **communication:** using language imaginatively
- **communication:** selecting vocabulary to create impact.

When authors write novels or short stories, they must give the reader a sense of where the action is happening. We call this the setting. It is an important part of building a picture in the reader's mind.

DRAFTING

1. Write a sentence or two describing your classroom. The sentences should not just list things you can see – they must convey your feelings about the room. Is it a lively and interesting place in which to learn? Or does it need brightening up?

2. Swap your writing with that of another student. What word would you choose to describe the feelings your partner has about the classroom? If you could improve their piece by changing one word, what word would it be?

READING

3. The author George Orwell is best known for his novels *1984* and *Animal Farm*, but he also wrote many non-fiction books. Read Source A, an extract from a book Orwell wrote about the living conditions in northern England just before the Second World War.

Source A

I remember a winter afternoon in the dreadful **environs** of Wigan. All round was the **lunar** landscape of slag-heaps, and to the north, through the passes, as it were, between the mountains of slag, you could see the factory chimneys sending out their plumes of smoke. The canal path was a mixture of cinders and frozen mud, criss-crossed by the imprints of **innumerable** clogs, and all round, as far as the slag-heaps in the distance, stretched the 'flashes' – pools of stagnant water that had seeped into the hollows caused by the **subsidence** of ancient pits. It was horribly cold. The 'flashes' were covered with ice the colour of raw **umber**, the bargemen were muffled to the eyes in sacks, the lock gates wore beards of ice. It seemed a world from which vegetation had been banished; nothing existed except smoke, shale, ice, mud, ashes, and foul water.

From *The Road to Wigan Pier* by George Orwell

Vocabulary

environs: surrounding area

lunar: like the moon

innumerable: too many to count

subsidence: when land sinks to a lower level

umber: a reddish-brown earth colour

DISCUSSING

4 Work with another student. Discuss these questions about the extract:

- **a** What does the line 'nothing existed except smoke, shale, ice, mud, ashes and foul water' suggest Orwell thinks about the landscape he is describing?
- **b** What are the connotations of each of the words in the line? For example what does 'ice' make you think of?

Watch Martin Phillips talk about how to describe a setting on Cambridge Elevate.

5 Choose another short section of the extract and explain to your partner how you think it presents a negative view of the scene.

EXTENDED WRITING

A writer's choice of words enables them to create a scene in the reader's mind. When a photographer takes a picture of a landscape, they also make choices that affect the way people viewing the image will respond to it. For example a colour photo of a field of sunflowers shot in golden light on a summer evening will feel very different from a black and white shot of a derelict housing estate in the middle of winter.

6 Choose one of the photographs in Source B, then select one or more of the words in the following word bank that you think best matches the mood created by the image.

lonely	serene	stressful	barren	deserted
desolate	bleak	enigmatic	wild	exotic
idyllic	epic	lush	nightmarish	intense
relaxing	awesome	communal	soothing	inhospitable
colourful	depressing	dilapidated	picturesque	

7 Plan a paragraph about the photo you chose from Source B. Aim to present a strong viewpoint about the landscape – as George Orwell does when writing about Wigan, for example. Decide which details you will write about to build this viewpoint and think carefully about the words you will use to describe the details.

8 Now write your paragraph of about 150 words. When you have finished, swap your work with another student. Suggest improvements to each other's writing.

Source B

Writing workshop 3

This is how to organise writing. No it isn't.

Your writing improvement focus for this workshop will be:

- **communication:** exploring an alternative approach to description and narrative
- **organisation:** using sentence variety to add effect
- **SPaG:** purposeful use of question marks and exclamation marks.

WRITING

1. Write a description of who you are in 8–10 sentences.
2. Work with another student and compare your writing. Make notes of similar details you mentioned – for example where you live, the colour of your hair, your height, and so on.

READING AND DISCUSSING

3. Read Source A.
4. With your partner, discuss what unusual approach the writer takes and compare this with your own descriptions from Activity 1. Whose do you think is most effective? Why?
5. Describe the various moods presented in this extract. Give examples to support your choices – for example 'the narrator seems aggressive and contradictory when …'.
6. Describe any points where you were surprised or shocked by the information that the character reveals.

Watch Mike Ferguson talk about taking risks with writing on Cambridge Elevate.

Source A

You don't know me.

Just for example, you think I'm upstairs in my room doing my homework. Wrong. I'm not in my room. I'm not doing my homework. And even if I were up in my room I wouldn't be doing my homework, so you'd still be wrong. And it's really not my room. It's your room because it's in your house. I just happen to live there right now. And it's really not my homework, because my math teacher, Mrs. Moonface, assigned it and she's going to check it so it's her homework.

Her name is not Mrs. Moonface, by the way. It's really Mrs. Garlic Breath. No it's not. It's really Mrs. Gabriel, but I just call her Mrs. Garlic Breath, except for the times when I call her Mrs. Moonface.

Confused? Deal with it.

You don't know me at all. You don't know the first thing about me. You don't know where I'm writing this from. You don't know what I look like. You have no power over me.

What do you think I look like? Skinny? Freckles? Wire-rimmed glasses over brown eyes? No, I don't think so. Better look again. Deeper. It's like a kaleidoscope, isn't it? One minute I'm short, the next minute tall, one minute I'm geeky, one minute **studly**, my shape constantly changes, and the only thing that stays constant is my brown eyes. Watching you.

That's right, I'm watching you right now sitting on the couch next to the man who is not my father, pretending to read a book that is not a book, waiting for him to pet you like a dog or stroke you like a cat. Let's be real, the man who is not my father isn't a very nice man. Not because he is not my father but because he hits me when you're not around, and he says if I tell you about it he'll really take care of me.

From *You Don't Know Me* by David Klass

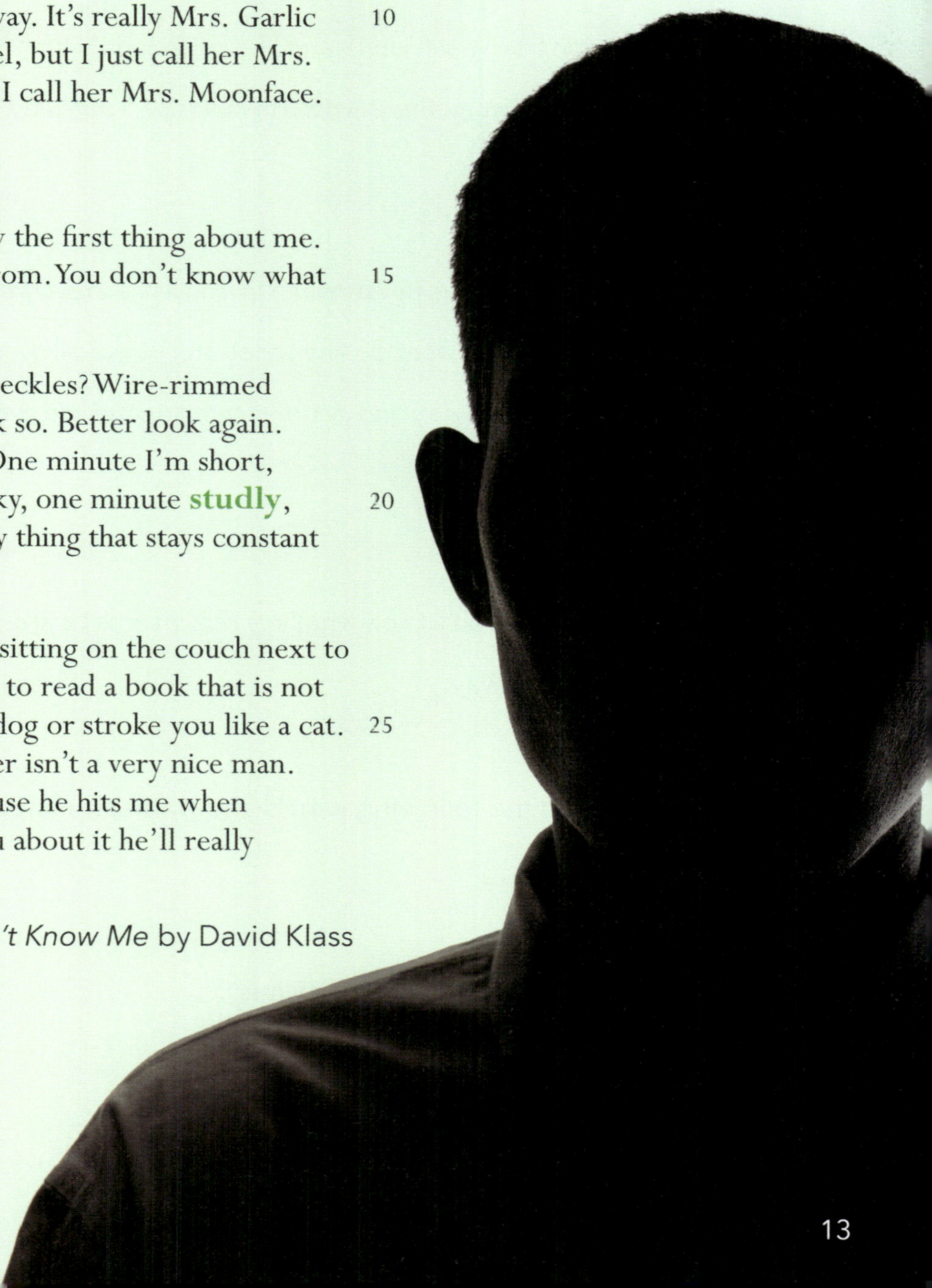

Vocabulary

studly: strong and manly (like a stud)

DRAFTING

7 Think about what you have learned through your discussion. Now begin drafting a similar contradictory narrative that describes yourself. It can be real or imaginary – or a combination of both. Choose more than one mood so that you shift from one to the other, from happy to sad, calm to angry, funny to grumpy, and so on.

To help you when drafting your own piece, read Source A again. The following example of a student's writing might also be a useful model:

I am an athlete. I can run the fastest 100 metres in my school. I can jump the highest. I have muscles that make the girls blush and the boys jealous. I am actually a secret superhero but I don't tell my friends and just make sure I am the best at sports but don't go over the top. For example when I'm in a race, I don't fly. When I throw the javelin, I don't launch it into space.

I'm not really a superhero. I've never held a javelin, let alone thrown one. When I ran the 400 metres I immediately went to the toilet and puked all over the place. I'm a couch potato. I sleep 12 hours a day and get my mum to drive me everywhere. I hate sports.

Confused? Get over it.

You don't know me. You don't know what my real interests are. You might not care, but I'm going to tell you anyway.

You might also find the following words and phrases useful:

- 'You don't know me'
- 'No/No I am not'
- 'No it isn't'
- 'That's not the case/that's not how it is'
- 'Of course it isn't'
- '… and now the … who is not my …'
- 'Deal with it'
- 'Get over it'
- Asking questions: 'So where am I?'

WRITING: REVIEW, EDIT AND FINAL VERSION

8 Before writing your final version, re-read your draft. Consider the following:

- **a** **Purpose:** check against your choice – is the writing about yourself entirely true or entirely false, or a combination of both? If it is a combination, is it balanced?
- **b** **Audience:** are there enough twists and turns to keep your reader guessing and entertained?
- **c** **Communication:** have you described how you look, what you like, things you have done, friends you have, places you have been, what you love about school, what you love about writing?
- **d** **Organisation:** have you avoided a simple pattern of statement/contradiction followed by statement/contradiction? Have you used a mixture of long and short sentences to add to the impact of a varied pattern of statements and contradictions?
- **e** **Accuracy:** you will probably have included many questions and exclamations in your contradictory description, so have you punctuated correctly with question marks and exclamation marks?

Try punctuating a piece of writing on Cambridge Elevate.

Writing workshop 4

Lists in a sentence

Your writing improvement focus for this workshop will be:

- **communication:** exploring the power of lists in writing
- **communication:** presenting a list of details for information or impact
- **organisation:** developing sentence structures for specific purposes
- **SPaG:** using appropriate in-sentence punctuation.

By the time you have completed the 'List' workshops, you will have explored the following: listing details; applying the list of three in a slogan; applying the list of three in a speech. You may even have created your own 'list poem'.

Did you notice that the previous paragraph was an example of listing details in a sentence? This, along with the following examples, will demonstrate the various purposes and effects of a list.

Watch Lemn Sissay talk about the power of sentences and punctuation on Cambridge Elevate.

DISCUSSING

1 Look at the following four examples of lists.

- **a** Work in pairs. Discuss and make notes on what you think is the **purpose** and **effect** of using a list in each of these four ways. Consider, for example, if every item in the list is presenting information to create a visual effect. If the writer has made a different choice, what is it and what is its effect?
- **b** What feelings (if any) are created by the use of a list in these examples?

Content list (comma separators)

1 Fluorescent pencil case, healthily filled lunch box, lucky soft-toy duckling, stuffed rucksack, kisses and hugs from Mum: Lucy was ready for her first day at school.

2 When John's dad opened his son's kit bag to collect dirty clothes for washing, he found: mud-splattered shorts, a mud-streaked jersey, mud-caked football boots, mud-filled socks and mud-smeared school exercise books that shouldn't have been left in the bottom of the bag!

Grammatical list (semi-colon separators)

3 In that one moment of decision, Sam had to consider the following: would he have the energy; would he have the courage; could he live with himself; could he ever return; should he change his mind?

4 When they reached the top of the hill they looked out amazed at the approaching storm clouds; the perfect blue sky before them; a sparrow-hawk flying towards the darkness; the valley below split half in light and half in shade; the river cutting between both sections; and a shared feeling of dread at what they knew was also going to happen later that day.

WRITING

2 Make notes on how the writer's choice of words is an important part of the overall effect created by the lists in the examples.

3 On your own, write at least two sentences with a 'content list' and at least two sentences with a 'grammatical list' similar to the examples given.

4 When you have finished writing, swap with another student and compare your lists. Together, decide on the best example of each type of list.

Writing workshop 5

Lists of three

Your writing improvement focus for this workshop will be:

- **communication:** exploring the power of lists in writing
- **communication:** using a list of three as a rhetorical device
- **organisation:** choosing words and phrases for impact on the reader
- **SPaG:** using in-sentence punctuation to support meaning.

The 'list of three' (or the 'rule of three') is a device that writers use for impact, especially in formal speech. The repetition of phrases with similar words, meanings or sounds creates an echoing effect that reinforces meaning:

That's the truth, the whole truth and nothing but the truth.

The list of three can be as simple as three adjectives in a sentence. However, using it in this way may not have much impact on the reader. Sentence variety is far more important.

The list of three can be a powerful rhetorical device. The word 'rhetorical' here means a method for creating impact. That impact is to strengthen the way a piece of writing informs, persuades and motivates an audience to react as a reader or listener.

DISCUSSING

1 Work with another student. Discuss the following examples of the list of three as single words or short phrases. Use these bullet points to focus your discussion:

- Which are **verb triples** (three action words) and which are **phrase triples** (three similar groups of words)?
- Repetition is common in lists of three. Are any other techniques or effects used?
- Make a note of exactly what you think each list is telling you to do, or just telling you.
- Describe the feeling or attitude of each list – what tone is used to get across the message?

a Stop, look and listen.
British public safety slogan

b Never before in the field of human conflict was so much owed by so many, to so few.
Sir Winston Churchill

c Slip! Slop! Slap! (Slip on a shirt, slop on some cream, slap on a hat.)
Australian public safety slogan

d Government of the people, by the people, for the people …
The Gettysburg Address

e The rule is: jam tomorrow, and jam yesterday, but never jam today.
From Through the Looking Glass *by Lewis Carroll*

DISCUSSING AND WRITING

2 Work in small groups. Create three **verb** slogans that suggest action for each subject. Select from the following ideas, or think of your own:

- **a** exam revision advice (think of the **prefix** 're-')
- **b** bicycle safety tips
- **c** environmental concerns
- **d** school dinners/canteen advice
- **e** tips on walking a dog
- **f** tips on stroking a tiger.

3 In the same groups, create three **phrase** slogans to raise awareness of the subject of each one. Select from the following ideas, or think of your own:

- **a** fast food joys/dangers
- **b** social media manners
- **c** sports activity promotion
- **d** impact of a music genre
- **e** talking not texting (or vice versa)
- **f** bullying.

READING

4 Read Sources A and B. Read the descriptions and think about how each source expands the list of three into separate sentences.

Source A is the closing two paragraphs from the long speech Nelson Mandela gave at his trial in South Africa in 1964. Notice how he uses repetition purposefully. The word 'struggle' is presented in a rule of three in the first paragraph, then repeated once more in the second; 'fought' is repeated twice and the key word 'ideal' is also given in a rule of three.

Vocabulary

ANC: African National Congress

Source A

This then is what the **ANC** is fighting. Their struggle is a truly national one. It is a struggle of the African people, inspired by their own suffering and their own experience. It is a struggle for the right to live.

During my lifetime I have dedicated myself to this struggle of the African people. I have fought against white domination, and I have fought against black domination. I have cherished the ideal of a democratic and free society in which all persons live together in harmony and with equal opportunities. It is an ideal which I hope to live for and to achieve. But if needs be, it is an ideal for which I am prepared to die.

From Nelson Mandela's 'I am prepared to die' speech

Source B is from Shakespeare's *Julius Caesar*. There are two famous speeches in this play – one delivered by Brutus and one by Mark Antony, after Caesar has been killed. Both speeches use repetition for powerful effect, trying to convince the Roman citizens, their audience, that they know what is best for Rome. At the end of Brutus's main speech, Shakespeare has him speak with a traditional, carefully structured rule of three.

Source B

Who is here so base that would be a bondman? If any, speak; for him have I offended. Who is here so rude that would not be a Roman? If any, speak; for him have I offended. Who is here so vile that will not love his country? If any, speak; for him have I offended. I pause for a reply.

From *Julius Caesar* by William Shakespeare

WRITING

5 Imagine you are going to make a formal speech. Think of a subject – this should be important, but the tone of your speech can be either serious or humorous. Write one paragraph for a key section of your speech, using a list of three.

If you need extra help, treat the extract in Source B as an exact model for your chosen subject. Come up with three **rhetorical questions** to ask (repeated exactly or with slight differences), then create balancing answers. For example:

Who here has had the salad instead of chips today? Well done, for you will be healthier in both body and mind. Who here has had fruit instead of cake today? Well done, for you will be fitter in both body and mind. Who here has had juice instead of soda today? Well done, for you will be less fizzy in both body and mind.

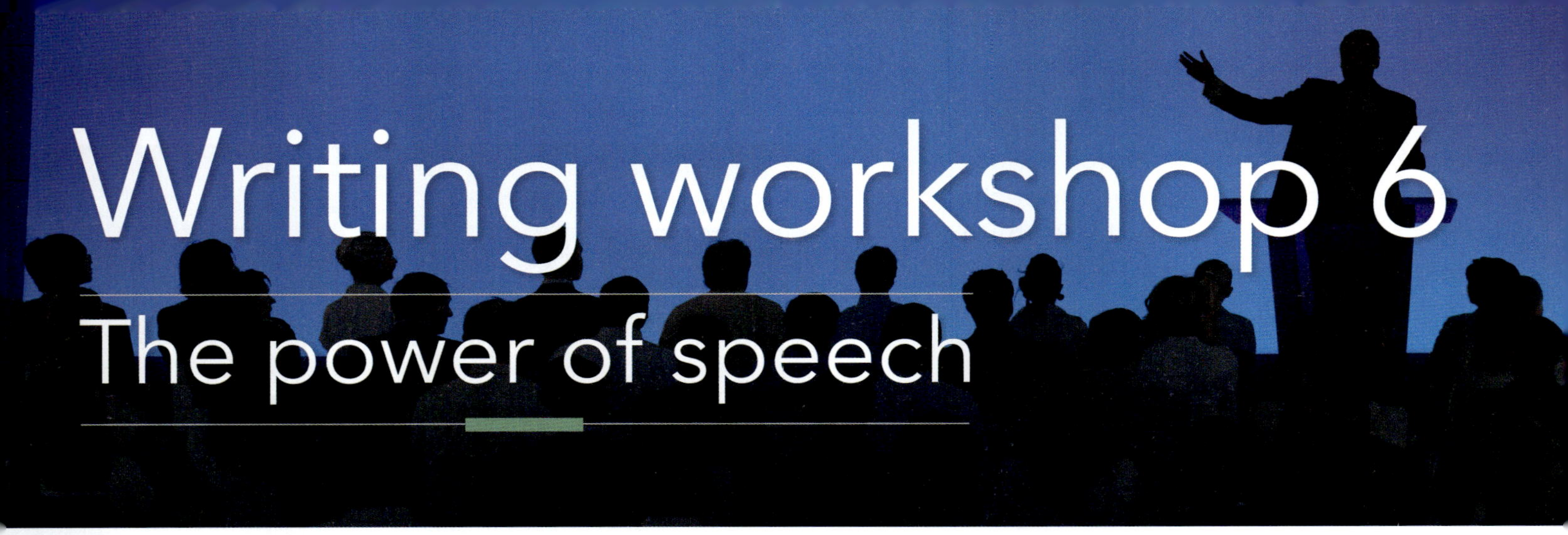

Writing workshop 6

The power of speech

Your writing improvement focus for this workshop will be:

- **communication:** writing an effective speech
- **communication:** organising ideas to persuade listeners to your point of view
- **spoken language:** build your skills in planning and giving a speech or presentation.

Being able to give a good speech is an important skill. Although some people can make a speech without much preparation, most people need to plan carefully what they are going to say. Many well-known speeches were written by professional speechwriters rather than the famous figures who delivered them. In this workshop, you will practise writing for the spoken voice.

American Civil Rights activist Angela Davis giving a powerful speech in 1974.

1 Zahraa is a Year 10 student. She has been asked to write the text for a speech persuading her peers not to smoke. What advice would you give Zahraa on how to write a successful speech?

READING AND DISCUSSING

2 Read Zahraa's first draft:

Personally, I think smoking is a filthy habit. It's becoming more and more common these days for children to be smoking. Who is influencing them? Is it us, the older children, or even adults? How are they buying these cigarettes? They are going into shops and shopkeepers are allowing them to buy them. Why is this happening? Is it all about the money? Do they know the consequences of smoking? Who's there to teach them? Nobody. I know this person, they smoked so much, their lungs got so black and tarred up they had to have a tube put in their throat to help them breathe properly. Do they know about this? Are they leaving it to the schools to teach them? What is going on? They're starting to smoke from the age of eight or even younger. Who's influencing them? Is it us the older children? Where are they getting this from? They're seeing their parents smoking and they're just coming to do it themselves. It needs to stop and it needs to stop today.

3 Work with another student:

a Talk about how successful you think Zahraa has been in drafting her speech.
b Decide on three things that might improve her work.

4 Look at the following list of rhetorical devices that are often used in formal speeches. Which ones does Zahraa use?

Rhetorical questions (questions intended to make someone think rather than expecting an answer):
How would you like to be cooped up in a tiny cage all your life?

Facts and statistics (to prove what you are saying):
80% of the people interviewed thought smoking bans in pubs were a good idea.

Emotive language (to make someone feel shocked or emotional):
Animals endure intense pain when their eyes are injected with poisonous chemicals to test perfume.

Use of personal pronouns such as 'I', 'you', 'us', 'we', 'our' (to make someone feel they are being spoken to directly):
We need to do something about this. I feel very strongly that together we can make a difference.

Flattery (to suggest that someone will feel good about themselves if they do something):
Of course, you wouldn't dream of blowing smoke all over a baby.

Lists of three (repeating something three times for impact):
Factory farming is cruel. Factory farming is immoral. Factory farming is therefore unacceptable.

Imperative sentences (those that begin with an imperative verb):
Do something about it!

Varied sentence lengths (using a few short, simple sentences):
Act now.

Personal anecdotes (examples of your own experiences):
My own sister was caught up in this shocking bullying.

Watch Lemn Sissay discuss the power of rhetorical devices on Cambridge Elevate.

DRAFTING

5 Now re-draft Zahraa's speech:

- **a** Break it into paragraphs. Each paragraph should have a clear topic.
- **b** Use a greater variety of rhetorical devices than Zahraa. Do not overdo it, but try to use an appropriate range from the list – at least one device in each paragraph.

6 With a partner, compare the changes you have made. Together, draft one paragraph that uses the best parts of each of your work.

WRITING: DRAFT, REVIEW, EDIT AND FINAL VERSION

7 You are going to write a speech to persuade people to donate to a charity of your choice. The speech will be used on one of the main television channels, just before the main evening news. It must fit into a two-and-a-half-minute slot. People speak at about three words per second, so your speech needs to be roughly 450 words long.

- **a** First, create a mind-map of all the things you think would help to persuade people to give generously to your charity. Do not worry about writing in full sentences – in fact, do not think too hard about each idea you put down. At this stage you want as many ideas as possible so that you can choose the best.
- **b** Look at all the ideas you have mapped and decide on the three or four that you think are the most powerful.
- **c** Write a first draft, taking a paragraph for each of the ideas you have chosen. Do not worry about spelling or punctuation yet – you will come back to check that at the end. Getting the ideas to flow is the most important thing at this stage.
- **d** You might already have used some of the rhetorical devices you looked at earlier. If not, see where you could introduce some of them to give your speech greater impact.
- **e** Check your spelling and punctuation and amend as necessary to make your speech as accurate as possible.
- **f** Finally, copy it out neatly or type it up as a finished version.

SELF-ASSESSING AND IMPROVING

The words you have written are obviously important, but when the script comes 'off the page', there are other things you need to think about in order to make it a powerful piece of spoken language. These include:

- volume
- **pace**
- emphasis
- **intonation**
- facial expressions.

8 Work with another student. Take it in turns to read your speech to each other. As you listen to your partner, make notes about the features in the list in order to help them improve.

9 Take your partner's comments into consideration. Then practise your speeches until you do not have to read from the script the whole time, but can make eye contact with your listener quite often.

PRESENTING

10 If you can, record a performance of your speech. You should set up the camera so that you are seen in mid-shot (waist upwards). Record your speech as many times as you need to until it is as good as it can possibly be, then share it with the class.

Writing workshop 7

Banning words

Your writing improvement focus for this workshop will be:

- **communication:** writing a formal letter to argue and persuade (ideas and language choices)
- **organisation:** presenting ideas clearly and concisely (purposeful paragraphs).

DISCUSSING

Watch Mike Ferguson talk about formal letters on Cambridge Elevate.

1 Think about when you might choose to speak in **formal language** rather than casual, **informal language**.

a Name three occasions when you would speak formally.
b Name three occasions when you would speak informally.

2 What differences are there between formal and informal language? Copy and complete the table to illustrate these two types of language in a job-interview situation.

Job interview: interviewee	Formal language	Informal language
saying hello	Good morning. Thank you for inviting me …	Hiya! How's it going today?
referring to qualifications		
referring to previous experience		
asking about salary		
referring to career plans		
saying goodbye		

3 You would normally use formal language in a job interview, as well as conforming to a formal dress code. In what kinds of jobs might you use informal language? Why?

READING, DISCUSSING AND PRESENTING

4 Read Source A, which is an extract from a newspaper article about formal and informal language.

5 The words that the academy banned are:

- 'coz'
- 'aint'
- 'like'
- 'bare'
- 'extra'
- 'innit'
- 'you woz'
- 'we woz'
- beginning sentences with 'basically'
- ending sentences with 'yeah'.

a Work in pairs or small groups. Discuss the ban of student words at this school. Decide on three reasons why someone might agree with the ban and three reasons why someone might disagree.

b Present your 'for' and 'against' decisions to the rest of the class.

6 Continue working in your pairs or groups:

a Make a list of ten words and phrases that you would ban from parent and/or teacher talk.

b Present your words and phrases to the rest of the class.

DRAFTING

7 Draft a formal letter to a newspaper agreeing or disagreeing with the ban discussed in Question 5. Include words that adults use when speaking to young people which you think should be banned. To support your opinion, include examples from the school's banned list as well as your own.

Source B is a template that you can use for this writing task and for any real formal letter in the future. Notice how the letter should be set out and what should go in each of its four paragraphs.

When writing a letter in an examination, you are usually expected to start with a salutation, or greeting (e.g. 'Dear Sir' or 'Dear Chris Elliot') and end with 'Yours faithfully' or 'Yours sincerely'. Use 'Yours faithfully' if your salutation is 'Dear Sir' or 'Dear Madam'. Use 'Yours sincerely' if your salutation is 'Dear' plus the person's name.

Source A

Students at Harris Academy Upper Norwood have been banned from using 10 informal phrases in school areas designated 'formal language zones', which includes all classrooms and corridors.

The initiative introduced in September, by the school's new principal Chris Everitt, hopes to raise awareness about the use of language and prepare students for formal situations such as job interviews.

From an article in *The Guardian* by Carmen Fishwick

If sending a formal email, you do not need to use addresses as presented here, but do include your address at the end.

10 Angry Road
Complainingshire
5ED UP

your address

Editor
The Guardian
Kings Place
90 York Way
London
N1 9GU

their name, or title/position if name unknown, and address

Dear Chris Elliot,
Dear Sir or Madam,

formal address if you don't know the person's name

I am writing in response to your article on the … and wish to make suggestions about the adult words I think should … .

Paragraph 1: explain simply your reason for writing.

The words young people use are … ; the words young people use as students are … , and the words adults use to speak to young people are … .

Paragraph 2: give the details of your complaint. Think about your writing choices (e.g. the 'list of three') when presenting your main ideas here.

The … parent or teacher words and phrases I would like banned are … . Choosing three of the worst offenders, as a young person I dislike … because … . I get upset about … because … and my third choice of … makes me so angry I … .

Paragraph 3: say what you would like done in response to your complaint.

Thank you for your consideration. I look forward to hearing from you.

Paragraph 4: close your letter simply and formally.

Yours sincerely, / Yours faithfully,

Yours sincerely: if you have named the person you are writing to

Yours faithfully: if you don't know the name of the person you are writing to

WRITING: REVIEW, EDIT AND FINAL VERSION

8 Now review and edit your letter. Consider the following:

- **a** **Purpose:** does it convey your opinion about language and attitudes to language?
- **b** **Audience:** does your own choice of language suit adults preferring a broadsheet to a tabloid newspaper?
- **c** **Content:** will your readers be engaged by what you have to say and how you say it? For example have you included interesting facts, **anecdotes** or appealed to your readers' experience?
- **d** **Expression:** as a formal letter, have you chosen your vocabulary and sentences to convey reasoning and awareness of different viewpoints? For example do your sentences balance statements with words such as 'possibly', 'maybe' or 'in some cases'?
- **e** **Organisation:** are your paragraphs purposeful? For example do they introduce, develop and conclude concisely?
- **f** **Accuracy:** are spelling, punctuation and grammar suitable for publication in a national newspaper?

Writing workshop 8

Don't stop the train 1

Your writing improvement focus for this workshop will be:

- **communication:** making choices about the type of sentences you use
- **communication:** matching vocabulary closely to the meaning of your writing.

Read Source A aloud.

Source A

Away, with a shriek, and a roar, and a rattle, from the town, burrowing among the dwellings of men and making the streets hum, flashing out into the meadows for a moment, mining in through the damp earth, booming on in darkness and heavy air, bursting out again into the sunny day so bright and wide; away, with a shriek, and a roar, and a rattle, through the fields, through the woods, through the corn, through the hay, through the chalk, through the mould, through the clay, through the rock, among objects close at hand and almost in the grasp, ever flying from the traveller, and a deceitful distance ever moving slowly within him.

From *Dombey and Son* by Charles Dickens

The expressive power of this paragraph comes from the use of repetition and the choice of vocabulary, especially verbs. The many short phrases, separated by commas, also convey sight and sound in what is being described. By discussing these, you will learn how word and sentence choices can have a significant impact in writing.

READING AND DISCUSSING

1 Read Source A again, then discuss the following questions with another student:

- **a** How do the rhythms of the sentences provide clues for the reader that the narrator is travelling on a train?
- **b** In your pairs, decide on the most noticeable thing about the writer's choice of sentence structures in the passage.
- **c** Make a list of five words or phrases that you think represent the sounds of the train effectively.

DISCUSSING AND WRITING

2 Work in pairs. Describe to your partner a journey by car, bus or train that you recall because you either did or did not enjoy the experience.

3 Write three sentences recording what you remember most about the journey.

Watch Mike Ferguson talk about the benefit of discussion on Cambridge Elevate.

READING AND DISCUSSING

4 Look at Source B – the next paragraph from the text. Read it aloud several times, listening for a rhythm to the words.

a What is the rhythm like – regular, fast, slow? Or does it change throughout? If so, where and how?
b Discuss how the sentence structure creates this rhythm.

Source B

Through the hallow, on the height, by the heath, by the orchard, by the park, by the garden, over the canal, across the river, where the sheep are feeding, where the mill is going, where the barge is floating, where the dead are lying, where the factory is smoking, where the stream is running, where the village clusters, where the great cathedral rises, where the bleak moor lies, and the wild breeze smoothes or ruffles it at its inconstant will; away, with a shriek, and a roar, and a rattle, and no trace to leave behind but dust and vapour.

From *Dombey and Son* by Charles Dickens

5 Take it in turns to read the paragraph aloud again, this time really focusing on the rhythm you have discussed.

PRESENTING

6 Look at Source C – the next paragraph from the text. In your pairs, divide up the paragraph between you. Be careful to choose the 'natural' places to swap reading. Then present the extract as a vocal double-act to the class.

Source C

Away, with a shriek, and a roar, and a rattle, plunging down into the earth again, and working on in such a storm of energy and perseverance, that amidst the darkness and whirlwind the motion seems reversed, and to tend furiously backward, until a ray of light upon the wet wall shows its surface flying past like a fierce stream. Away once more into the day, and through the day, with a shrill yell of exultation, roaring, rattling, tearing on, spurning everything with its dark breath, sometimes pausing for a minute where a crowd of faces are, that in a minute more are not; sometimes lapping water greedily, and before the spout at which it drinks has ceased to drip upon the ground, shrieking, roaring, rattling through the purple distance!

From *Dombey and Son* by Charles Dickens

INTERPRETING

7 Work in three groups.

- **a** Using a copy of one of the three paragraphs you have been reading, highlight the nouns and the verbs in different colours.
- **b** As you work on your paragraph, choose ten of Dickens's nouns and verbs and present them as a colour-coded collage.

Access the extracts from *Dombey and Son* in full on Cambridge Elevate.

8 Display the posters in the same order as the paragraphs to represent the complete motion of the train in the extract.

PRESENTING

9 Perform a whole-class rendition of one, two or three of the paragraphs. This will require a choral discipline that needs some time to practise!

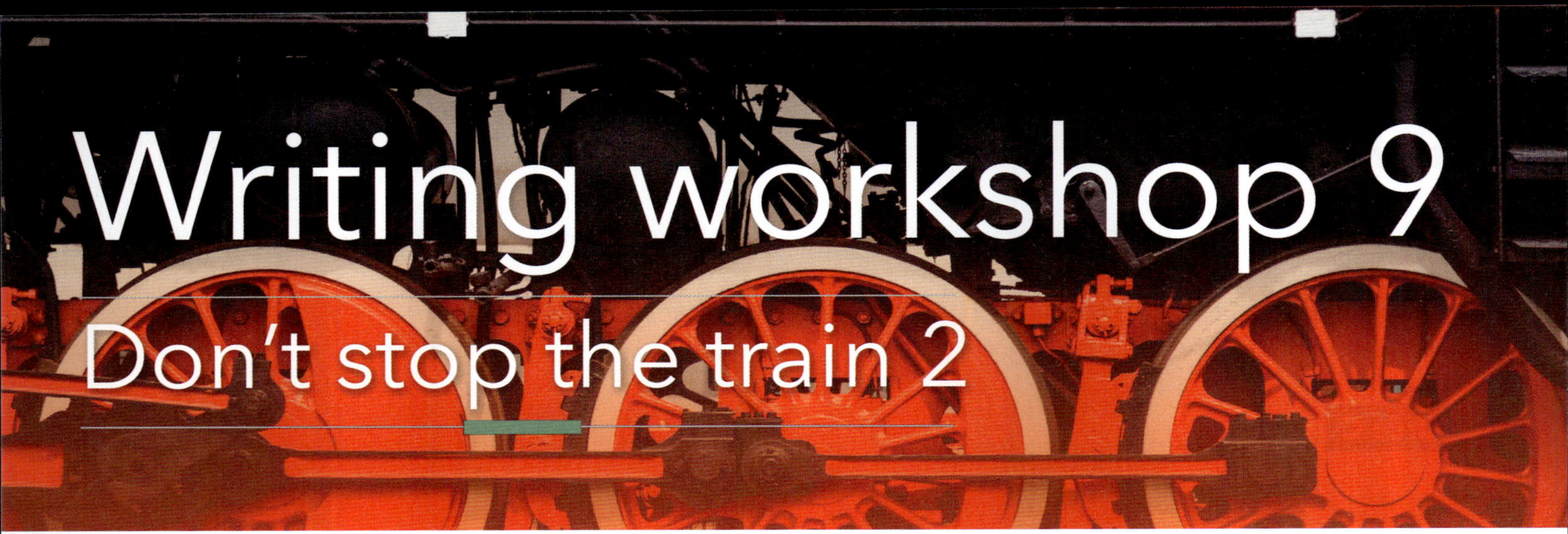

Writing workshop 9

Don't stop the train 2

Your writing improvement focus for this workshop will be:

- **communication:** making choices about the type of sentences you use
- **communication:** matching vocabulary closely to the meaning of your writing.

Source A

At Fordsburg station our train was on the point of departure. We scrambled on. The train moved off. The engine puffed and screamed a shrill warning. We found a place near the window. The woman sat on the hard wooden seat. I stood with my nose pressed against the dirty windowpane, watching the world go by.

The engine puffed and snorted. Every now and then, when the train curved round a bend, it screamed its shrill warning. And the wheels, under me, whispered: "O-n a-w-a-y. O-n a-w-a-y. O-n a-w-a-y." Then they said: "On away. On away. On away." Then they said: "On away, on away, on away." And after that, for nearly all the time, they said: "Onawayonawayonawayonawayonawayonawayonaway."

Soon the houses and other buildings were far behind. The land came rushing up, only to rush away again: vast stretches of green land, and brown land; land rising and falling. Sometimes hills and mountains flashed by. Sometimes we went through a mountain and were in darkness. And the engine would scream its warning and we would come out of the mountain. Tall telegraph poles came up to meet us, then rushed away with clock-like regularity. And all the time the wheels said: "Onawayonawayonawayonawayonawayonawayonawayonawayonaway," till I was drunk with it all.

From *Tell Freedom* by Peter Abrahams

READING AND DISCUSSING

1. Read Source A, an extract from a novel by the South African author Peter Abrahams.

2. Work with another student. Compare Source A with the passages by Charles Dickens in Workshop 8. What similarities are there? What are the differences? Think about each writer's choice of words and sentence structures.

3. In your pairs, read the passage aloud, with each of you taking different sections. Is it easier or more difficult to find places to swap voices than it was for the previous extract?

PLANNING

You are going to write a paragraph using similar sentence and vocabulary choices as those in the extracts by Dickens and Abrahams. In your paragraph, you should try to capture the sight, sound and movement of a journey and/or mode of transport by your word and sentence choices.

4. Choose one of the following examples you may have experienced or want to imagine for your writing:

   a an aeroplane (perhaps taking off)
   b a car going onto the motorway, or negotiating small country lanes
   c a Formula 1 racing car in a race on a track, or a repetitive circular banger race
   d a motorbike roaring up through the gears or a scrambler on a dirt track in the woods
   e a skateboard in a skateboard park (think of the specific sounds here)
   f any other noisy mode of transport.

5 Prepare to write by creating a word bank of nouns appropriate to your chosen journey and mode of transport. Then create a verb bank to convey the appropriate motion and sound. To describe a skateboard in a skateboard park, for example, your word banks might look like this:

Nouns

deck	lapper	regular	riders
trucks	nose guard	half pipe	rails
wheels	tail guard	quarter pipe	switch
grip tape	tail devil	handrails	pools
bearings	copers	funboxes	
ribs	half pipe	vent ramps	
sliptape	goofy	bowls	

Verbs

grinding	manoeuvring	grating	popping
turning	backsliding	falling	frontsliding
sliding	nosegrinding	bruising	carving
bumping	flipping	crashing	
skidding	tailsliding	rolling	

(The '-ing' ending can create a sense of movement because it adds an extra syllable; however, you can also use active verbs such as 'grind', 'slide', 'pop', and so on.)

WRITING

6 Now write your paragraph describing a journey in a particular mode of transport. Develop your ideas, your details, vocabulary and sentence structure so that readers will gain a strong impression of the movement of your vehicle.

7 Swap your writing with that of another student. Using two different coloured highlighter pens, mark any parts of your partner's writing that show features adapted from the two published writers you have studied in these two workshops.

PRESENTING

8 With your partner, prepare to read each finished piece to the rest of the class. When one person has read either all or a part of their writing aloud, the other should comment on one or two aspects that have been developed through the work in these units.

Writing workshop 10

Language bites

Your writing improvement focus for this workshop will be:

- **communication:** using words creatively and imaginatively in printed advertisements.

Printed advertisements have very little time to grab your attention. Whether they are on a page in a magazine or mounted on a billboard, they are fighting for attention with all sorts of other things around them. The pictures and the words must both be powerful and arresting.

The image is often the most important part of an advert, but the words help to fix a meaning in the reader's mind. The words often stay with people long after the images have faded. Sometimes they take on a life of their own. Twenty years ago, an advertising agency came up with a slogan for Ronseal woodstain: 'It does exactly what it says on the tin'. In 2013, Prime Minister David Cameron used the same phrase to describe a government agreement, saying: 'It is a Ronseal deal – it does what it says on the tin.'

DISCUSSING

1. Work in pairs or small groups. List as many advertising slogans as you can. Try to come up with ones from the past as well as the present.

2. Imagine you are creatives in an advertising agency (the people who come up with the ideas for adverts). Your agency specialises in healthy-living campaigns. You have been hired by the Department of Health to produce a poster campaign to convince people to cut down on drinking alcohol. You have been provided with an image, Source A, showing a lifeless hand holding an empty bottle.

   Work in your groups to come up with a powerful slogan to accompany the image.

Source A

WRITING

3 The poster campaign you designed has been a great success. The Department of Health has now commissioned you to create a radio advertisement as a follow-up.

Work on your own. Write the script for a 30-second advertisement. You can use no more than 100 words, so every word counts! Your advert should end with the slogan you wrote for the poster. Source B shows an example script for you to use as a model.

PRESENTING

4 Make a recording of your finished advertisement. You will need to recruit 'actors' to read each part. Make sure you encourage those who read the script to make it interesting by varying their expression. Ask them to think about their intonation. You will need to hold your listeners' attention throughout if they are to buy into your message.

Source B

SOUND:

RESTAURANT NOISES - PLATES, CUTLERY, WAITERS/WAITRESSES TAKING ORDERS.

MAN: So what are you going to order? The menu looks great.

WOMAN: I'm not sure. I think I'll have vegetable soup followed by a green salad and wholewheat roll.

MAN: You mean you're not going to have the cheesy garlic bread and lasagne?

WOMAN: No. I'm trying to eat my five portions of fruit and vegetables every day and to cut down on my fat intake.

MAN: Surely you can have something you like every now and then?

WOMAN: Yes, but I worry that I'll slip into my old ways if I'm not careful.

MAN: Hmmm. This looks interesting. It was clipped to the menu.

WOMAN: 'FOOD STEPS: A guide for people who want to eat more healthily'. Sounds like me!

MAN: It's free and everything is mailed to you. No gimmicks and no meetings to attend either!

ANNOUNCER: FOOD STEPS is new and unique. FOOD STEPS: we truly understand the way you want to eat.

Writing workshop 11

Pitching in

Your writing improvement focus for this workshop will be:

- **communication:** writing a document for an advertising agency to persuade a client to buy your services (ideas and language choice)
- **organisation:** presenting ideas persuasively (purposeful paragraphs).

Source A

LIGHTNIN' SHOES UK

MARKETING BRIEF

Jason Sole,
Senior Marketing Executive
Lightnin' Shoes UK

Our trainers are losing market share to our rivals. We need a campaign that will reposition our brand and increase our percentage of the market.

Our target audience is predominantly male, aged between 16 and 24:

- They will have an active lifestyle, preferring to be out on the streets rather than playing computer games.
- Music plays a big part in their lives.
- They are acutely fashion conscious: wearing the right brand is very important to them.

Your agency is invited to make a pitch outlining ideas in three areas:

1. a storyboard for a 30-second TV advertisement that presents Lightnin' trainers in an exciting way
2. a poster campaign to support the TV advertisement
3. ways of using social media to draw attention to the campaign.

As we have approached a number of agencies, your initial pitch will need to be short and focused. It should consist of:

- a spoken presentation, lasting no longer than three minutes, which explains clearly what you are proposing
- a written response to this brief, of no more than 450 words, which explains clearly what you intend to produce and why you think it will sell more of our trainers.

You are going to prepare a presentation to the marketing department of a company that manufactures sports gear, so that they will choose your idea for an advertisement. This is called a pitch.

READING

1. Read the brief (Source A) that the company has sent you. This outlines what they need from the new marketing campaign.

DISCUSSING AND PRESENTING

2. Work in groups of three or four:

   a Discuss ideas that you could suggest to Lightnin' during the spoken pitch. Make sure you have strong ideas for all three of the areas they have identified in the brief. You should work out: why your ideas will work; language choices such as slogans and key words; music choice; which social media and how you will use them, and so on.

   b Decide who is going to present each section in a live pitch.

3. When you are ready, present your ideas to the rest of the class.

WRITING

4. You have heard a lot of different ideas for how to improve the sales of Lightnin' trainers. Now you are going to write your own response to the brief to send to Lightnin' Shoes UK.

   You can choose any ideas from any of the group presentations. The important thing is to make your writing powerful and persuasive. Above all, you must make it clear to the marketing executive exactly what you are proposing.

Use this example for help or prompts if you need to:

Make an opening statement (this should clearly and quickly say what you are trying to do):

Today's trainer market is a crowded place. Lightnin' Shoes are fighting for recognition against many high-profile brands. Our campaign will give you a niche that sets you apart from the competition.

Develop your points:

You can see from the images we have presented that we are going for a street-smart sense of casual style …

Wrap up your pitch:

With all these ideas, you can see that we are going to ensure that Lightnin' Shoes hit the spot.

Watch Tom Phillips describe how to design and deliver an advertising pitch on Cambridge Elevate.

Writing workshop 12

Instruct and advise with style

Your writing improvement focus for this workshop will be:

- **communication:** adapting a particular style for your writing advice
- **communication:** choosing appropriate imperatives for instructing
- **organisation:** presenting instructions in chronological order.

The publishers of a writing project called 'Understanding Teen Tasks' are commissioning short articles for a variety of magazines aimed at parents of teenagers. You have been asked to provide an article for one of these magazines.

The aim of the project is to help parents understand the interests and activities of their teenage children by producing a range of serious to not-so-serious articles about these interests. The publisher wants the articles to be written in a style similar to cookbooks by celebrity chefs. They hope that this will be an unusual and engaging way of advising and instructing adults on typical teenager tasks.

DISCUSSING

1 Work in small groups. Discuss the following topics and decide which 'teen task' you will write your article about:

- **a** negotiate with parents to stay out extra late one evening
- **b** save all data and change a phone SIM card
- **c** paint your bedroom in a favourite football team's colours
- **d** dye your hair
- **e** upload music to SoundCloud, YouTube or similar
- **f** code a new Tumblr theme
- **g** upload street-style photos to your blog
- **h** repair a bicycle puncture
- **i** create a homework diary spreadsheet
- **j** set up a themed Facebook page
- **k** any similar task of your choice.

WRITING

In any recipe or instruction manual, the key form of language used is the **imperative**. In recipes, for example, this will usually be the imperative verbs such as 'pour', 'chop', 'slice', 'add', 'put', and so on.

2 Work on your own. As quickly as you can, write down ten imperatives, similar to those listed, which you could use to give instructions for your chosen task.

3 Now swap your list with another student who has chosen to write about the same task as you. Compare your choice of imperatives. Note words that both of you chose and also those that only one of you chose.

4 Together, agree on five new imperatives for your task and write them down.

READING

5 You are going to base the style of writing in your article on that of television chef Nigella Lawson. Read Source A, an extract from one of her recipe books.

DISCUSSING

6 In small groups, discuss Nigella Lawson's writing style in Source A:

a How are word choices such as 'kitsch in the kitchen', 'unchic', 'smuggery', 'gorgeously garish' and 'textural heaven' typical of her writing style?

b How is the organisation of the following sentence also typical of her writing style?

This is exceptionally good, a taste sensation and textural heaven; bite into it and savour a finely balanced contrast – tender, poached meat within, crisp coating seared onto it – that the great names of the old Nouvelle Cuisine could only dream of … .

WRITING

7 Now write your article about how to instruct and advise on your teenage task. Organise your writing into two clear paragraphs:

a The first paragraph should be about advising how to collect all the materials/tools/ideas needed for the task, as well as how to organise them in the most sensible way according to the order in which they are used. Use a similar style to Nigella Lawson's - celebrate and boast about the positive purpose of the task you are about to undertake!

b The second paragraph should include the task instructions, using precise but varied imperatives throughout. Make sure that the instructions are believable. Present these in the correct order to successfully complete the task. You can exaggerate the style-model of Nigella Lawson to add humour and engage your adult reader.

Read a recipe on Cambridge Elevate.

Source A

Enjoying food, enjoying eating, isn't about graduating with honours from the Good Taste university ... Yes, I want whatever I do eat to be good, but there is surely a place – and in my heart a very fond one – for a bit of kitsch in the kitchen ...

SOUTHERN-STYLE CHICKEN

There's something about frying, especially in vegetable shortening and in such Rosanne-like quantities, that is so refreshingly unchic. But I assure you there's no element of let's-go-slumming smuggery about the inclusion of this recipe here, for all the glee I take in the gorgeously garish wrapper in which my vegetable fat of choice comes. This is exceptionally good, a taste sensation and textural heaven; bite into it and savour a finely balanced contrast – tender, poached meat within, crisp coating seared onto it – that the great names of the old Nouvelle Cuisine could only dream of ...

Put the chicken pieces in a dish into which they fit snugly. Pour over the milk to cover and sprinkle over the tablespoon of salt. Dibble with your fingers to mix in. Cover with clingfilm and leave in the fridge for a few hours or overnight.

From *Nigella Bites* by Nigella Lawson

Writing workshop 13

Create drama and suspense

Your writing improvement focus for this workshop will be:

- **communication:** writing a short narrative to create drama and suspense for the reader
- **organisation:** selecting vocabulary and use grammatical structures to create suspense.

An image can create drama and suspense because we 'read' the visual clues. What clues can you find in the following image?

READING

1 Writers use language clues to create drama and suspense. Read Source A, an extract from a novel. A police raid is described to create drama in the action as well as suspense about the surprise and outcome of the raid for both the main character, Callum, and the reader.

Source A

There was no warning. No knock at the door. No warning shouts. Nothing. The first I knew about it was the CRASH when our front door was battered in. Shouts. Calls. A scream. Footsteps charging. Doors banging. More shouts. More footsteps – pound, pound, pound up the stairs. By the time I was fully awake and had swung my legs out of bed, smoke was everywhere. At least I thought it was smoke. I dropped to the floor.

'Jude? JUDE!' I yelled, terrified that my brother was still asleep. I jumped up, looking around for him.

It was only then that I realized it wasn't smoke filling my room, filling the house. The strong smell of garlic caught in the back of my throat and brought instant tears to my eyes. I coughed and coughed, my lungs threatening to explode from my body and my eyes were streaming. *Tear gas*. I struggled to my feet and groped my way to the front door.

'DOWN! GET DOWN!' A voice, no, more than one voice, screamed at me.

I turned in the direction of the voice, only to be pushed to my knees, then down to the ground. My chin hit the hard floor, making me bite down on my tongue. My arms were jerked behind my body. Hands bent back. Cold, hard steel cutting into my wrists. My eyes hurt. My lungs hurt. My tongue hurt. I was pulled to my knees, then yanked up. Pushed and pulled and punched forward. I couldn't see. I closed my burning eyes – and I admit, I was crying by now, trying to clear the tear gas, desperate to stop the pain. My lungs were being filed with sandpaper. Stop breathing. Just stop. But I couldn't. And each breath was strong as ammonia, sharp as a razor.

'JUDE! MUM! DAD!' I called out, only to choke over the words. Only to choke. I couldn't take much more. My body began to seize up, curl in on itself. And suddenly we were out. Out of the house. Out into the cool, night air. I tried to draw a breath. My lungs were being sliced. I gasped. More air – clean, fresh air. Just as I was pushed into the back of a car, I heard my mum crying.

'MUM!' I called. I blinked, and blinked again, looking around, trying to see her. Shapes and shadows swam before me. The car took off. My hands were still handcuffed behind my back. My whole body hurt.

And I still didn't know why.

From *Noughts and Crosses* by Malorie Blackman

PRESENTING

2 Work in groups of at least four. Produce a dramatic reading of Source A, emphasising the increasing drama and suspense.

- **a** One of you should read Callum's **dialogue**, one the raider's dialogue and others alternating paragraphs or the narrative.
- **b** Pay particular attention to the sentence structures and language repetitions. Think about how these suggest ways to read the piece.

3 When you are ready, make your presentation to the class.

DISCUSSING

4 Using what you have learned from listening to other groups' readings, discuss the techniques the writer uses to build drama and create suspense. Think about:

- **a** the situation Callum is in
- **b** Callum's minimal dialogue
- **c** the sentence structure
- **d** the choice of repeated words and phrases
- **e** techniques such as the use of **alliteration** and **metaphor**.

DRAFTING

5 Choose one of the following scenarios:

- **a** You have gone for a walk in a forest. You suddenly realise that you have not been concentrating on the route you have taken and are now lost. It is getting dark.
- **b** You are walking home late at night. You suddenly hear footsteps quite close behind you. You think they are following you. In fact, they seem to be getting closer … .
- **c** You are in a lift that is stuck between floors. You have already been in it for more than an hour. The temperature is rising and it is getting unbearably hot. You think you can smell smoke.

6 Draft your own short narrative (no more than 200 words) to create drama and suspense for your reader. When drafting your piece, consider the following points:

a Impact on the reader – does the narrative:
- begin by clearly setting the dramatic scene?
- move through distinct stages, building suspense?
- have an effective ending?

b Other things to consider:
- **Purpose:** has the piece built up tension and suspense effectively?
- **Audience:** does the choice of language vividly convey a sense of fear to the reader?
- **Organisation:** are the paragraphs purposeful (do they introduce, develop and conclude)?
- **SPaG:** are punctuation and sentence structure used in an interesting way to help create suspense?

Watch Alison Clink describe how she plans her short stories on Cambridge Elevate.

WRITING: PEER-ASSESSING AND IMPROVING

7 Swap your work with another student. Read your partner's narrative and give them written feedback. Use the points listed in Question 6 as the headings for your feedback.

Writing workshop 14

It was a dark and stormy sentence

Your writing improvement focus for this workshop will be:

- **communication:** avoiding over-writing in sentences by reducing adjectives, metaphors and similes.

There is an annual 'bad' writing competition called the Bulwer-Lytton Fiction Contest. Entrants submit, for fun, their intentionally worst-written sentence for consideration. The competition was inspired by the following extract from a novel by Edward George Bulwer-Lytton:

It was a dark and stormy night; the rain fell in torrents – except at occasional intervals, when it was checked by a violent gust of wind which swept up the streets (for it is in London that our scene lies), rattling along the housetops, and fiercely agitating the scanty flame of the lamps that struggled against the darkness.

From *Paul Clifford* by Edward George Bulwer-Lytton

DISCUSSING

1 Work in groups. Discuss the reasons why this sentence is not a good description by asking yourselves questions about how effective the details and vocabulary really are:

- **a** What level of light do you expect at 'night'?
- **b** If it is 'stormy', how would rain be falling?
- **c** Could this storm and wind exist in any city, or just London?
- **d** What is wrong with the phrase 'fiercely agitating the scanty flame'?

DISCUSSING AND PRACTISING

In exams, students often try too hard in their writing and use too many language devices. Two examples of this are:

- the overuse of adjectives – especially in a single sentence
- the overuse of metaphors and **similes**.

2 In your groups, look at these attempts by a student to improve the following sentence:

He walked into the room.

He walked nervously into the darkened room.

He walked nervously, like a frightened deer in a prairie full of wolves, into the dark and dismal room that was dimly lit by some mean and milky moonlight.

He edged into the gloomy room.

a Work out what the student changed when rewriting each sentence.
b Which version is most effective? Why?

3 Now produce your own examples of overwriting and then improving a **simple sentence**. Try at least two of the following:

a He tripped on the stone.
b She looked at the door.
c They held onto the rope.
d They turned off the alarm.

Watch Mike Ferguson discuss the dangers of overwriting on Cambridge Elevate.

DISCUSSING

4 Look at the two rewritten versions of Bulwer-Lytton's sentence. After reading each one, discuss the questions that follow. They will help you consider how, sometimes, 'less is more' in good writing.

It was a wild night. The rain did not stop. The wind, roaring in gusts, fought the fall of the rain but did not win.

a Read the first two sentences aloud. How are they balanced?
b What single adjective is used, and why is this effective?
c What else makes this description work well?

It was a wild night. The rain did not stop. The wind, roaring in gusts, fought the fall of the rain but did not win. However, it did race up the road to shake a streetlamp, knocking out the light.

d How is the wind **personified**?
e What is the central metaphor in the sentence?

DRAFTING

5 Rewrite the following exaggerated sentences. Get rid of any unnecessary adjectives, metaphors and similes.

a The old man grasped tightly the hot coffee mug with his old wrinkled and creased hands.
b In the black dark of night the moon shone as brightly as a star in the distance, blinking like an eye as the clouds danced energetically across its beam of light.
c Sprinting like a runner, he raced to the shops to buy the lush delicious chocolate he desperately craved.
d The knuckles on his hands were knotted and bent like the upturned roots of a huge tree, and his shoulders hunched over his body like a grey stone bridge over troubled water.
e Deep in the depths of the wood a cold and icy-blue river chilled his heart in the eager anticipation of swimming in its fluid flow.
f The annoying sentence shouted out like a wailing baby having a temper tantrum as it repeated itself again and again with an excess of too many words.

WRITING

Correcting the exaggerated sentences in Question 5 is a light-hearted exercise in improving obvious overwriting. The serious challenge is to write vividly using the fewest, best-chosen words. This comes with practice – and wanting to improve.

6 Take three or four of your improved sentences from Question 5 and shape these into a coherent descriptive paragraph. You can add whatever extra detail you choose to craft this into a meaningful piece of writing.

Writing workshop 15

Pete can't speak, but you can

Your writing improvement focus for this workshop will be:

- **communication:** using dialogue to reveal and develop character in a story
- **SPaG:** learning simple rules for writing dialogue accurately.

In my view, stories and novels consist of three parts: narration, which moves the story from point A to point B and finally to point Z; description, which creates a sensory reality for the reader; and dialogue, which brings characters to life through their speech.

From *On Writing* by Stephen King

READING

1 Read Source A, an extract from the novel *Lean on Pete* by American writer Willy Vlautin. Fifteen-year-old Charley is estranged from his single-parent father and works looking after horses, including one called Pete. When the owner, Del, decides that Pete will be taken to Mexico and sold for meat, Charley steals a truck and trailer and runs away with the horse. But then an elderly driver crashes into them, badly injuring Pete.

- **a** Have different people reading Charley's dialogue, the policeman's dialogue and the narrative.
- **b** As you read or listen, think about how the feelings of Charley and the policeman are revealed by their dialogue.

Source A

A police car came. Its lights flashed in the darkness. An officer got out of the car and went to the old woman and asked her questions, then walked over to me.

'Are you alright?' he asked.

I shook my head.

'Are you hurt?'

I shook my head.

'Is this your horse?'

'No,' I said barely. 'He's his own horse.'

The policeman went back to the old woman and talked to her and she went to her truck and started it. It took a while but she got it going. One of her headlights was out, her hood was crushed, and her windshield was cracked all over. The engine didn't sound right, but she moved it to the side of the road. The officer used his radio and called for a tow truck, then told them about Pete and he spoke on the radio asking for a tractor and a flatbed truck. He came over to me.

'Can you stand up?' he asked. 'Can you walk over to the car?'

'I can't leave Pete,' I said.

'Pete's the horse?'

I nodded.

'Where do you live?'

'I don't know.'

'Where's your family?'

'Don't know.'

'What's your name?'

'Charley Thompson,' I said.

'Where did you used to live?'

'Portland,' I told him.

'Okay,' he said. 'Just stay here, alright?'

I nodded and he went back to the police car and he was there for a long time. When he came back he shined the flashlight in my face.

'Did you steal a truck and trailer? Did you steal this horse?'

I just held on to Pete. I didn't say anything.

'Are you that Charley Thompson?'

I nodded.

The flashlight was pointing right at my face and he wouldn't take it away.

'I didn't mean to,' I said. 'Del was going to send him to Mexico. I know he was.'

'Del's the owner of the horse?'

'Yeah.'

'Where were you heading?'

'Wyoming.'

'What's in Wyoming?'

'My aunt,' I said and started crying.

'So, you're a runaway?'

'No,' I told him.

'Where are your parents?'

'I don't know,' I said.

The officer looked at me for a while. He wasn't mad, he had a kind voice. 'We'll take you in and get you cleaned up. We'll figure out what's going on. Okay?'

'Okay,' I said.

Pete's head was lying on the asphalt. His tongue was hanging out. There was blood everywhere and you could see his broken leg bent up towards his neck.

From *Lean on Pete* by Willy Vlautin

DISCUSSING

2 Work with another student. Discuss the following questions:

- **a** How do you know immediately that the policeman isn't angry?
- **b** What does Charley's response 'He's his own horse' (line 8) suggest about how he is feeling when it is said?
- **c** What adverb does the writer use to convey Charley's true feelings when saying the above? How does this work?
- **d** What simple punctuation marks tell the reader that Charley is not angry when he repeats twice 'I don't know' to the policeman's questions?
- **e** What narrative details are added to the dialogue between Charley and the policeman near the end of the extract to support what we know of how each is feeling through their speech?

Watch Willy Vlautin talk about writing dialogue on Cambridge Elevate.

PRACTISING

There are specific rules you must stick to when punctuating speech.

Every word that is spoken should be placed inside speech marks:

'I'm speaking this so it has to be inside speech marks.'

When a new and/or another person speaks, this must start on a new line:

'I'm speaking this so it has to be inside speech marks,' I said.
'Well, I'm talking too so I get my own speech marks and a start on a new line,' he insisted.

There must always be a punctuation mark at the end of speech, whether it is a comma, a full stop, a question mark or an exclamation mark:

'I'm speaking this so it has to be inside speech marks,' I explained.
'Do I get my own speech marks?' she asked hopefully.
'I wish you would listen to what I just said!' I shouted.
'Just asking.'

All narrative details that come before, after or in between speech must be punctuated accurately:

'I'm speaking this so it has to be inside speech marks,' I explained.
Yawning, she replied, 'I know, you've already told everyone again and again.'
'I'm just trying to be helpful,' I moaned, 'so there's no reason to be so rude!'
'You think that's rude?' she spat, whilst storming out of the room.

3 The dialogue in Source A is dramatic but calm. Take a section and re-present it as angry and loud. Use adverbs and adverbial phrases around speech and appropriate punctuation marks to convey this.

PUNCTUATING

Punctuate the extract on Cambridge Elevate.

4 Look at the following extract, which comes earlier in the novel. It explains how Charley is able to drive the truck and trailer. The punctuation is not all correct. Copy out the passage, punctuating it accurately.

Del drove past them and up to a big barn and shut off the engine. We got out and uploaded the horses and I followed him inside the barn and we put them in the stalls. Do you know how to drive? Sort of, I said. You know how to work a clutch? My dad's truck has a clutch. He lets me drive him around sometimes. This one's tricky. I'll be okay, I said. Alright, he said and handed me the keys. Take the truck and trailer down the road away from the house, park it, then clean the muck out the trailer. There's a shovel and a broom in the bed of my truck. Then come find me. I nodded and he walked up towards the house and I got back in the truck and started it. The clutch was going out. I stalled it six or seven times before I finally drove down to where he said and parked it.

EXTENDED WRITING

Immediately after the end of the extract in Source A, Charley runs off into a field and escapes into the darkness of the night.

5 Write the next part of the story, using a significant amount of dialogue to continue to reveal Charley's feelings and those of any other characters you include. You can imagine your own situation or choose from the following:

- **a** The policeman finds Charley and coaxes him to return with him to the police station. Use the dialogue between the two to continue the care and concern shown by the policeman, as well as Charley's reluctance to reveal much about his situation.
- **b** The same as above, but change the mood of the policeman. Or change Charley's mood so that he reveals more about why he decided to steal Pete with Del's truck and trailer.
- **c** In the novel, Charley sleeps rough the night he escapes from the policeman and the next day he hitches a ride with a man who speaks through a box in his throat (caused by smoking cigarettes). He is a bit grumpy, but friendly, and he quizzes Charley about who he is and where he is going. He also warns Charley not to smoke and not to do anything else that's bad for him, like watching too much TV! Write this conversation. How would Charley handle this stranger? Would he confide or continue to be protective about his situation?

Writing workshop 16

In someone else's shoes

Your writing improvement focus for this workshop will be:

- **communication:** writing imaginatively
- **organisation:** maintaining coherence and consistency across a text.

At the heart of all good novels and short stories are well-developed characters. You might be intrigued by them or repelled by them, but for you to want to read on, the writer must bring them alive.

Watch Alison Clink discuss how to 'show not tell' on Cambridge Elevate.

PREPARING

1. Choose one of the following four images to work with. Note down answers to the list of questions that follow, from the point of view of the character in the image you have chosen.

- **a** What's your name?
- **b** How old are you?
- **c** How are you feeling at the moment?
- **d** Where would you rather be?
- **e** What do you dream of doing?
- **f** What worries you?
- **g** What would you like others to think of you?
- **h** What keeps you awake at night?
- **i** What is the best thing you ever did?
- **j** What is the worst thing you ever did?
- **k** How would you like to be remembered?
- **l** What phrase or saying do you often use?

2 Now choose one of the objects from the following list. You are going to write a **first-person monologue**, in role as your character, telling your reader about a life-changing event that has happened to you. The object you choose must play an important part in the monologue.

- **a** a broken video camera
- **b** an African mask
- **c** a blood-stained shirt
- **d** a rusty nail
- **e** a highly polished stone
- **f** a stopwatch
- **g** a framed photograph of a child and a dog
- **h** a cigarette lighter
- **i** a badge saying 'No more war'
- **j** a programme from a football match
- **k** a train ticket
- **l** a pair of pearl earrings
- **m** a peacock feather
- **n** a child's toy
- **o** an object of your own choice

3. Quickly note down all the ideas you can think of that might be developed in your final piece of writing. Do not think too hard about each idea yet – the point of this activity is to get as much onto paper as you can. Once you have a lot of ideas to work with, then you can start to shape and develop them.

PLANNING

4. The next stage is to decide which are the strongest ideas in your notes. You are going to write about 400 words and probably use five or six paragraphs. Think about which idea each paragraph could deal with and jot these down in a numbered list.

DRAFTING

5. Using your plan as a guide, draft your monologue. At this stage, concentrate on developing the narrative as powerfully as you can. As you are writing, remember your three choices:

Choice 1: Word choices. What words am I going to use to help my reader picture and imagine things clearly?

Choice 2: Sentence structure. How can I craft each sentence to create suitable effects (such as suggesting the character's emotion, building suspense, and so on) to engage my reader?

Choice 3: Text structure. How can I build my whole piece of writing so that it takes my reader on a logical or exciting journey through what I want to say?

EDITING

6. The final stage of the writing process is to go back and look carefully at what you have written. After you have considered the points below, make amendments to your writing as necessary.

a Have a look at your first sentence: what questions will it raise in your reader's mind, drawing them in and making them want to read on?

b Are there any words you could change to increase the impact of your writing on the reader?

c Is the punctuation accurate? Does it make your meaning clear to your reader? Are there any sentences that you could punctuate in a different way to make a clearer impression?

In exam conditions, you will not have the same amount of time as you have probably spent on this workshop. However, even in an exam it can be useful to follow a similar process to the one you have used here. Allow time for four stages:

- preparing
- planning
- drafting
- editing.

Writing workshop 17

Which side are you on?

Your writing improvement focus for this workshop will be:

- **communication:** exploring viewpoints and perspectives in texts
- **communication:** writing from a given viewpoint.

There is a saying that there are two sides to every story. However, when you read a newspaper or watch the news on television, you do not always hear both sides. When journalists write stories, they will often choose from a variety of information and present the story from a particular viewpoint to influence their readers.

One example is the way in which news organisations report on immigration to the UK. In January 2014, Romania and Bulgaria joined the European Union. This gave their citizens the right to come to Britain to work. Some newspapers took the viewpoint that this was a threat and warned of a 'wave' of perhaps millions of immigrants who might come here and take 'our' jobs.

DISCUSSING

Work in pairs or small groups. Look at the six photographs, taken at a trade unions demonstration protesting about government cuts to public services such as transport, schools and hospitals.

1. Decide which photographs could be used to support these different views:

   a the demonstration was peaceful and good-natured
   b the demonstration was a violent and destructive event.

2. Explain clearly to each other what it is about the photographs that makes you think it could be used for or against the protesters.

DRAFTING

3 Imagine you are the picture editor of a national newspaper. You have received an email from the editor explaining that the paper will be running a front-page story about this 'violent' demonstration against the government. She has attached the six photographs and asked you to select the one you think most powerfully portrays the demonstrators as unruly lawbreakers.

- **a** Write a 50-word email to the editor explaining which photograph you have chosen and why.
- **b** Write a caption of 8–12 words that could be used to help readers see the image in the way you intend.

4 Do the same activity again, but this time as the picture editor of a newspaper that wants to give the viewpoint that the demonstration was peaceful and good-natured.

Watch Wendy Buckingham talk about sources and viewpoints in journalism on Cambridge Elevate.

WRITING

5 You are now going to take on the role of the journalist who will write up the story to accompany the photograph selected by the picture editor.

- **a** First, decide the viewpoint you are going to take in your article.
- **b** Read Sources A and B, the press releases from the trade unions and the Metropolitan Police. Choose appropriate sections and quotations to use which give the perspective on the event your newspaper wants to portray. Do not use more than 40 words in total from the press releases.
- **c** Write a 400-word article giving an account of the demonstration from your chosen perspective.

Source A

PRESS RELEASE

issued by the

Metropolitan Police Communications Office

Officers of the Metropolitan Police were faced with a major incident in central London today. Although relatively small in number – only 13,500 demonstrators took part in the protest – the violent tactics used by trade unionists stretched the force to capacity in defending property and keeping members of the general public safe.

'The same pattern we have seen in recent anti-government demonstrations emerged again today', said Deputy Commissioner Derek Denley, officer in command of the Special Patrol Group (SPaG) who policed the event. 'They say they are here to draw attention to things the government are doing which they don't like, but I am afraid their actions tell a different story. They seem hell-bent on causing as much damage as they can and intimidating law-abiding Londoners in the process.'

A significant number of buildings were seriously damaged by marauding crowds who smashed the windows of banks and shops. Officers of SPaG had to put on riot gear and forcibly contain the worst elements of the crowd into small areas, but not before three officers received head wounds from bricks thrown from the crowd into the police lines.

Source B

PRESS RELEASE

issued by the

Trade Union Congress

The TUC successfully brought 35,000 members – predominantly public-sector employees like teachers, nurses, and transport workers – to the capital today to demonstrate the widespread public anger at the government's spending cuts.

'It was all going really well, with our members marching in an orderly fashion along the route we had agreed with the police and the Mayor's Office,' said Alison Andrews, TUC Communications Officer. 'Unfortunately a few members of an anarchist group infiltrated the march and made a nuisance of themselves. They had nothing to do with the TUC and indeed it was our members who pointed them out to the police, urging them to arrest them.'

Overall, the march passed off peacefully, despite provocation from some of the officers of the SPaG. TUC members were jostled and shoved about, with some actually being penned into an area by Kensington Gardens and prevented from rejoining the main march. It was noticeable that, while TUC protesters were carrying placards and dressed in their ordinary clothing, the SPaG arrived wearing full battle gear. It is a shame that the Metropolitan Police, themselves the victims of savage cuts to staffing levels under this government's austerity programme, should inflame a situation which they are supposed to control by over-reacting in the way they did today.

But despite this unfortunate side show, the day of action showed how the workforce of the country are simply not prepared to allow schools, hospitals and transport services to be vandalised by the government.

Glossary

adjective a word used to enhance the meaning of a noun

adverb a word that adds to the meaning of a verb, adjective or another adverb (e.g. 'guiltily', 'easily')

alliteration repetition of the initial letter in adjacent words (e.g. 'dark, dank dungeon')

anecdote a personal story

audience the intended readers of a piece of writing

connotation an additional associated meaning of a word

dialogue a conversation, or part of a conversation, in a piece of writing

emotive language using language to influence how a person feels

first person the form of a verb or pronoun used when you are speaking or writing about yourself

formal language the type of language you would use in official situations or when talking or writing to someone you do not know well

informal language the type of language you may use with people you know well such as friends and family

imperative a verb form used to issue a command, often used with an exclamation mark (e.g. 'Listen!', 'Stop!')

intonation the rise and fall of the pitch of the voice when speaking

metaphor a word or phrase that describes one thing as something else

monologue a long speech given by one person (as opposed to dialogue, which is speech between two or more people)

noun a word that refers to a person, place or thing

pace the perceived speed of a piece of writing or speech

personification giving human qualities to non-human things

prefix a group of letters placed at the beginning of a word to change or modify its meaning

pronoun a word that replaces, or is used in place of a noun phrase

purpose the reason a piece of writing has been written

rhetorical question a question that is asked for effect rather than to obtain information

simile a comparison using 'as' or 'like' (e.g. 'She was like a fish out of water.')

simple sentence a sentence consisting of a single main clause

tone the mood or attitude the writer conveys in a piece of writing

verb a word that conveys an action in a sentence

Acknowledgements

The authors and publishers acknowledge the following sources of copyright material and are grateful for the permissions granted. While every effort has been made, it has not always been possible to identify the sources of all the material used, or to trace all copyright holders. If any omissions are brought to our notice, we will be happy to include the appropriate acknowledgements on reprinting.

p. 4 Cambridge Dictionary; p. 5 The Ernest Hemingway Foundation; p. 10 *The Road To Wigan Pier* by George Orwell (Copyright © George Orwell, 1937) Reprinted by permission of Bill Hamilton as the Literary Executor of the Estate of the Late Sonia Brownell Orwell and Penguin Books Ltd and Harcourt Brace & Co.; p. 13 Penguin Books Ltd; p. 20 The Nelson Mandela Foundation; p. 27 Copyright Guardian News & Media Ltd 2013; p. 32 Faber and Faber; p. 41 The Random House Group and Ed Victor Ltd; p. 43 The Random House Group; p. 49 Headline Publishing Group; pp. 50–51 Faber & Faber and HarperCollins Inc.; p. 53 Faber & Faber and HarperCollins Inc.

Picture credits

p. 6 (t) Donato/Shutterstock; p. 6 (b) John Pitcher/Thinkstock; p. 7 (t & b) Stefan Chabluk; p. 8 (t) gk-6mt/Thinkstock; p. 8 (bl) Bettmann/Corbis; p. 8 (bm) Janine Wiedel Photolibrary/ Alamy; p. 8 (br) Matt Gibson/Thinkstock; p. 9 Idphotoro/Shutterstock; p. 10 Bert Hardy Advertising Archive/Getty Images; p. 11 (l) Gordon Esler/Getty Images; p. 11 (r) federicofoto/Thinkstock; p. 12 Xtock Images/Thinkstock; p. 13 Hlib Shabashnyi/ Thinkstock; p. 15 Elnur/Shutterstock; p. 16 Chorniy10/Shutterstock; p. 17 (t) Superstock/ Alamy; p. 17 (b) Matt Tilghman/Shutterstock; p. 18 (t) TimArbaev/Thinkstock; p. 18 (b) petejeff/Thinkstock; p. 20 Pictorial Press Ltd/Alamy; p. 21 Donald Cooper/Photostage; p. 22 (t) Rawpixel/Shutterstock; p. 22 (b) Everett Collection Historical/Alamy; p. 23 alessandro0770/Thinkstock; p. 26 ArtFamily/Shutterstock; p. 27 Arcaid Images/Alamy; p. 29 stokkete/Thinkstock; p. 30 Science & Society Picture Library/Getty Images; p. 32 Zagrean Viorel/Shutterstock; p. 33 Evans/Thinkstock; p. 34 Sarah Jessup/Thinkstock; p. 35 (t) Michael Dunlea/Alamy; p. 35 (b) Edw/Shutterstock; p. 36 hobbit/Shutterstock; p. 37 (t) luckyraccoon/Thinkstock; p. 37 (b) Luna Vandoorne/Shutterstock; p. 39 (t) Pinkyone/Shutterstock; p. 39 (b) rekemp/Thinkstock; p. 41 Paul Brighton/Thinkstock; p. 42 (t) AnastasiaRasstrigina/Thinkstock; p. 42 (b) Pictorial Press Ltd./Alamy; p. 43 Antonio Scorza/Shutterstock; p. 45 andreiuc88/Shutterstock; p. 46 (t) Mike Rogal/Shutterstock; p. 46 (b) Nyvlt-art/Shutterstock; p. 47 InnervisionArt/Shutterstock; p. 48 GSPhotography/ Shutterstock; p. 49 (t) Schmidt_Alex/Shutterstock; p. 49 (b) Pictorial Press Ltd./Alamy; p. 51 Little_Desire/Shutterstock; p. 53 Wil Tilroe-Otte/Shutterstock; p. 55 (t) Kamila Starzycka/Shutterstock; p. 55 (bl) pinkhappy/Thinkstock; p. 55 (br) Photodisc/Thinkstock; p. 56 (l) Pictorial Press Ltd./Alamy; p. 56 (r) Phil Rees/Rex Features; p. 58 jerry2313/ Thinkstock; p. 59 (all) Emma Phillips.

Produced for Cambridge University Press by

White-Thomson Publishing
+44 (0)843 208 7460
www.wtpub.co.uk

Managing editor: Sonya Newland
Designer: Clare Nicholas